*P*etrified Forest National Park is a colorful land set in the arid country of northeastern Arizona. Spread beneath turquoise skies, the clay, sand and rock are aglow with shades of red and gold, barely hidden by the sparse cover of grass and spiny shrubs. For thousands of years, it has been home to various groups of people—some hunters, some farmers, but all tied to the vagaries of this harsh land.

These colorful badlands harbor many remnants of the past. Logs turned to stone, fossil bones, and other traces of life speak of times hundreds of millions of years past.

Petrified Forest National Park, located in northeastern Arizona, was established in 1962 to protect multicolored stone trees, Indian petroglyphs, and portions of the Painted Desert.

Front cover: "Old Faithful" log, photo by Dick Dietrich. Inside front cover: Sunrise below Kachina Point, photo by Jeff Gnass. Page 1: Anasazi petroglyphs on Newspaper Rock, photo by Fred Hirschmann. Pages 2/3: Longlogs Trail and Puerco Ridge, photo by Gail Bandini. Pages 4/5: Balanced logs atop Blue Mesa, photo by Jack Dykinga.

Edited by Cheri C. Madison.
Book design by K.C. DenDooven.

Third Printing, 1996
in pictures PETRIFIED FOREST The Continuing Story
© 1991 KC PUBLICATIONS, INC.

LC 91-60041. ISBN 0-88714-056-4.

in pictures
Petrified Forest
The Continuing Story®

by Lori and Carl Bowman

Carl Bowman received his B.A. in biology from New Mexico State University. He began his National Park Service career in 1974, and later served as Petrified Forest's Resource Management Specialist. Lori Bowman, with a degree in Park and Recreation Areas Management from Kansas State University, was with the National Park Service for ten years and also served at Petrified Forest.

FRED HIRSCHMANN

*Na*tional park areas
are special landscapes set aside
by acts of Congress to protect
and preserve features of national
significance that are generally
categorized as scenic, scientific,
historical, and recreational.
As Americans, we are
joint caretakers of
these unique places,
and we gladly share them with
visitors from around the world.

Although drawn by the lure
of colorful petrified logs and
fossil bones, visitors to
Petrified Forest can find
much more preserved within
this national park.
Archaeological sites and rock
art are abundant, wildlife
thrives on native grasslands,
and spectacular views of the
Painted Desert offer an
escape from the rush of the
highway. This unusual land
can be harsh and
unforgiving, but it also offers
the patient observer beauty,
quiet, solitude, and a chance
to study and relate to the
natural world of which we
are all a part.

*Puerco Indian Ruin is one
of many ruins left by the
Western Pueblo People
who once made this land
their home.*

7

GARY LADD

▲ **By its presence here on Blue Mesa, petrified wood speaks of change and invites further** questions. Trees of this size cannot grow here today. What climatic changes have occurred over the last 225 million years? What other fossils from that distant past are preserved here? Perhaps the most common question: "Why did these trees 'turn to stone'?" Why then and not now? Why here and not everywhere? How can we put the pieces together and describe something so ancient, so foreign?

8

A Forest That Was . . .

Petrified logs sprawl across the desert, hinting of a vastly different time. But these logs are only part of the story, just as trees are only part of the forest. Paleontologists studying these barren hills have discovered an amazing variety of fossils. With these fascinating relics, they are piecing together the story of a distant time, called the Triassic Period, about 225 million years ago. During the Triassic, Petrified Forest was full of slow-moving streams, swamps, and floodplains. Fish filled the waters, feeding on clams, plants, and each other. In turn, they fell prey to crocodile-like phytosaurs and giant amphibians called metopasaurs. The riverbanks were cloaked with ferns and cycads, while towering conifers grew on more distant hills. A bewildering variety of armored and ox-like reptiles browsed through this lush growth or dug up roots and tubers to eat. Insects darted through the air, pursued by gliding lizards, while larger predators lurked in the undergrowth. Important changes were taking place. Small dinosaurs were appearing. Though still dominated by their larger, more primitive relatives, they were the heralds of the next order. The Age of the Dinosaurs was near. Today we know the petrified logs are but part of this fascinating story. Today's visitor faces the challenge of seeing the forest *and* the trees.

▲ **O**nyx Bridge, like other fossilized remains, helps scientists portray the Triassic world of 225 million years ago. Abundant deposits of petrified wood define the scene as a semitropical forest. Less abundant are the bones, the leaf impressions, the scales, teeth and shells, that fill the gaps in the picture. Combining these bits of evidence, scientists are piecing together an exciting story in the drama of life on our planet.

Petrification ▷
occurred many times in
the petrified forest.
Each time, the
chemical environment
varied slightly, and the
resulting wood took on
a different appearance.
In some pieces, the
petrification process
faithfully preserved the
woody structures of the
logs, down to the grain,
down even to the
individual cells.

In their pure ▷
state, the quartz
minerals encasing
the wood are
relatively colorless.
But traces of iron
and manganese
stain the
microscopic
crystals into a
rainbow of colors.
Thus, colors do not
result from the type
of wood, but from
the chemistry of the
petrifying
groundwater.

GAIL BANDINI

How Wood Turns to Stone

From a living tree to semiprecious stone, fossilization seems like magic. But the magic of petrification is just the magic of chemistry. Like any chemical reaction, petrification starts with raw ingredients: wood, water, and mud. The wood was from primitive conifers that tumbled and battered their way downstream. This driftwood came to rest at the bottom of the murky waters in what is now Petrified Forest and was quickly buried by mud and sand. It was the mud that was the real key to petrification. Not just any mud would do. These ancient muds contained volcanic ash, belched from volcanoes to the south and west. The volcanic ash decomposed, releasing chemicals into the water. As the water seeped through the buried logs, these chemicals reacted to the wood, and tiny crystals began forming. Little by little, the crystals grew, encasing the wood and turning the trees to stone. As the chemical magic of petrification worked on, the streams added more mud and sand, burying the logs beneath hundreds of feet of sediment, where they were protected from the ravages of time and decay.

BETTY GROSKIN

△ **P**etrification has happened repeatedly around the world and throughout geologic time. Petrified Forest National Park is not unique in having petrified wood, but in having it in such colorful abundance. Indeed, the park's most common petrified wood, *Araucarioxylon arizonicum,* has been officially named the State Fossil of Arizona.

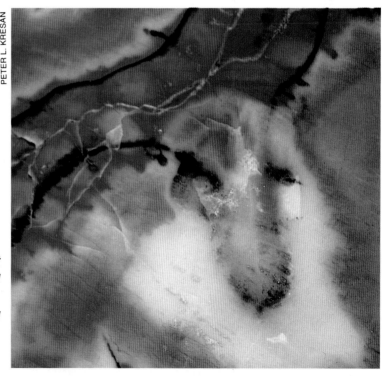

PETER L. KRESAN

Petrification begins as microscopic ▷ quartz crystals form in the wood cells, but sometimes crystals grow outside the cell walls, imparting new patterns to the wood. Later, other chemicals may enter cracks and fissures in the petrified wood, adding still more color.

Triassic Remains

◁ **The mud, sand,** and volcanic ash that buried and petrified the remains of Triassic creatures today form the rocks of the Painted Desert. Just as impurities color the petrified wood, they also tint the clays many different hues, including the soft blues and grays seen here at Blue Mesa. As these clays erode, they reveal harder rocks buried within, including the treasured fossil remains from the ancient Triassic forests.

DICK DIETRICH

The Life of a Log

◁ **Though buried for** millions of years, the petrified logs were still changing. Pressures within the Earth lifted this land over a mile above sea level, causing the logs to crack.

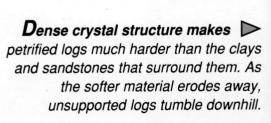 ▲ **Occasionally small streams** cut away soft sediments from under a much harder petrified log. If the balance of the log is just right, it may maintain its position and form a natural bridge like this one below the Painted Desert rim.

Dense crystal structure makes ▷ petrified logs much harder than the clays and sandstones that surround them. As the softer material erodes away, unsupported logs tumble downhill.

△ **A**s its name implies, Keystone Arch is "locked" in place by the shape of its sections. Just the right combination of the log's weight and shape have combined with a wash that is large enough to erode, but not destroy, this natural bridge. Given time and an undisturbed setting, the forces of erosion can produce many unusual, and fragile, forms.

Sometimes petrified logs shield ▷ the softer rocks beneath them. As the rains wash away the surrounding material, the log may be left high on a pedestal. But erosion is relentless, and the log's precarious perch is only temporary. This pedestal log at Blue Mesa fell in May, 1983.

When the Logs Come Tumbling Down

JOSEF MUENCH

△ **P**etrified wood may be broken apart by nature, and by human nature. The ancient people used petrified wood for tools, flaking off pieces as they needed them. Turn-of-the-century gem hunters used dynamite to open the logs and expose the crystals that lay hidden inside.

Petrified wood is extremely hard; indeed, ▷ it is harder than steel. But it is also quite brittle and can shatter like glass. As erosion uncovers the logs, it begins attacking them. The first attack may be from gravity as the logs tumble from an eroding mesa, battering each other on their way down. After millions of years, erosion may reduce the logs to grains of sand.

Small chips of petrified wood may form during the ▷ winter. Water seeps into cracks in the logs during the warm days, then freezes solid at night. Each time the water freezes it expands, forcing the crack wider until eventually, a piece of petrified wood flakes off.

Stresses cracked the
petrified logs even before they
were exposed. In flatter
areas, the pieces may stay
together as they are
uncovered. At Long Logs,
the length of these logs
helps us imagine the size
of the tall trees.

◁ **I**n the badlands, individual log
sections tend to roll down the steep
slopes as soon as they are
uncovered. At Jasper Forest these
petrified log sections lie scattered
across the desert floor.

18

Fate of the Logs

KENT & DONNA DANNEN

*T*he petrification ▷
*process that created these
logs ended hundreds of
millions of years ago, but
nature continues to shape
them. Here, plant roots help
to widen the cracks in a log.*

▽ **T*he abundance of petrified wood seen in Petrified Forest National Park is both impressive and*
*deceiving. Although the amount seems inexhaustible, petrified wood is, in fact, a limited resource.
Erosion continues to uncover new logs, but most of the petrified wood in the park is already exposed.
Nature has done her part in creating this colorful window on the past. The responsibility is now ours to
preserve what nature has provided. You can do your part by leaving each piece where you find it.*

A Land of Other Fossils, Too

A casual visitor to Petrified Forest might be excused for thinking that petrified wood is the only kind of fossil found in the park. Although amazingly abundant, petrified wood accounts for only three out of the hundreds of different fossil plant and animal species that have been discovered in these colorful clay hills and sandstone ledges. Delicate compressions of fern leaves, petrified bones, fish scales, clam shells, stem casts of giant scouring rushes, burrows, tracks, and many other kinds of fossils have given scientists an unparalleled view of life in this area 225 million years ago. Indeed, the various types of fossils found in this petrified forest combine to provide detailed information, not only about the individual plants and animals, but about their interrelationships, their habitats, the climate, and the topography. From this information, we are better able to understand the factors that ushered in the Age of the Dinosaurs.

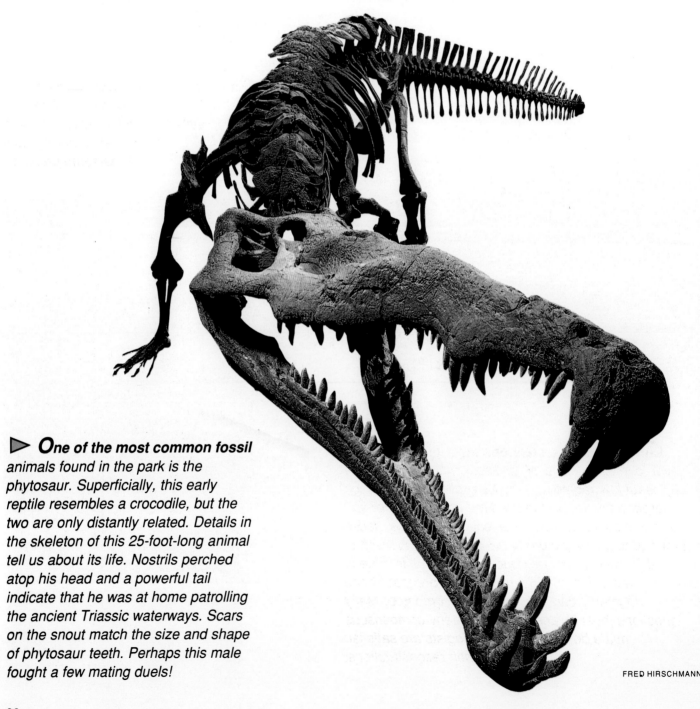

▷ **One of the most common fossil** animals found in the park is the phytosaur. Superficially, this early reptile resembles a crocodile, but the two are only distantly related. Details in the skeleton of this 25-foot-long animal tell us about its life. Nostrils perched atop his head and a powerful tail indicate that he was at home patrolling the ancient Triassic waterways. Scars on the snout match the size and shape of phytosaur teeth. Perhaps this male fought a few mating duels!

FRED HIRSCHMANN

Although details of the skeleton △
tell us Postosuchus was not a dinosaur,
slim, agile legs and a heavy skull with
sharp teeth show it was a
fearsome predator.

Complete fossil skeletons are almost △ ▷
never found in the field. Most discoveries are like these
phytosaur jaw fragments: tantalizing glimpses of a much
larger animal. Like the blind men and the elephant,
paleontologists use the clues contained in the pieces
they find to form a picture of the entire animal. Much of
this work cannot be done in the field. It is done in
laboratories and museums, where fossil bone
fragments can be studied and compared. Many
questions must be answered and many comparisons
made before the paleontologists are satisfied
by their reconstructions.

In the Field

__P__aleontologists ▷
scour the park looking for new fossils. Although they have a general idea of where to look, finding fossils is never easy. Erosion constantly uncovers new specimens, but most are just tiny fragments that the untrained eye would dismiss as just another piece of gravel.

◁ *__T__his cylindrical cast of a giant scouring rush is not petrified. Its hollow stem probably broke off during a flood, allowing the interior of the stem to fill with mud, thus preserving the shape of the plant. Comparing this specimen with its modern relatives, the horsetails, shows it to be a giant. Its stem is over ten times as wide as a modern horsetail. Today's horsetails are moisture-loving plants. This implies a stream-side home for the Triassic giant, an idea supported by the sandstone ripplemarks found nearby.*

△ **Although they may prospect the hills alone in their search for new** *fossils, scientists cannot work in a vacuum. Their work is better when it builds on and expands upon the findings of others. To promote this spirit of cooperation, paleontologists often sponsor joint field trips to important sites so they can share their expertise in sleuthing out clues from the ancient environment. A mix of scientists with different specialties and experiences, gathered in the field where the evidence is close at hand, helps to unravel perplexing problems. After the field and laboratory work are complete, the paleontologists' discoveries are published in scientific journals and eventually become part of our common knowledge. In Petrified Forest, the park staff talks with the paleontologists and uses journals to gather the latest information so it can be presented to park visitors. To guard against loss of the fossils and the information they represent, all scientists gathering fossils in the park must work under a permit. The fossils they find remain part of the park collections and are available for future study or public display.*

O*verleaf: Frozen in time,* ▷
*a pedestal log balances at Blue
Mesa. Photo by Fred
Hirschmann.*

A Real Detective Story!

▲ **Flash floods may wash fossil fragments far** from their original resting places. Paleontologists try to trace the fragments back to their source with the hope of finding other pieces still covered by a protective layer of rock. Complete skeletons are rarely found, but the more pieces paleontologists can find, the better their chances of determining the kind of animal they belonged to. Some of the most elusive fossils are the tiny bones of the fingers and toes. Yet even the tiniest fragments may shed new light on a subject.

◁ **Scraps of fossil bone mixed in with other** rocks on the desert floor are easily overlooked. But to the paleontologist, they are the beginning of a real detective story, one that leads from deserts to university laboratories. Before the story is finished, evidence from all over the world may be checked to identify the animal, perhaps new to science.

◁ **F**ossils must be carefully packaged for shipment. Usually, this means a big plaster cast. Once in the laboratory (here, outside the Painted Desert Visitor Center), the cast is opened and the encasing rock patiently chipped away, flake by flake, to reveal the bones within. This can be the most difficult part of paleontology (and the most expensive!).

Close study of the cleaned fossil ▽ offers information on joints, muscle attachments, size, and many other details. Since the bones are petrified, they may be too heavy or fragile to reassemble. In this case, a resin cast was made, allowing reassembly and study of an entire phytosaur in three dimensions.

FRED HIRSCHMANN

The Painted Desert

The Painted Desert and the Petrified Forest are really one and the same. They display the same rock layers, support the same plants and animals, and contain similar fossils including "forests" of petrified wood. The difference is simply one of focus. The focus of the Petrified Forest is close, looking at individual logs and fossils. The focus of the Painted Desert is on a grand scale. The vast expanse of sky and land, the bewildering topography, and the intense colors are what will be remembered. The Painted Desert is actually a large arc sweeping

_P_ilot Rock, in the northwestern △
_corner of the park, presides over the Painted
Desert landscape. On clear days the pastel
hues of the desert shine, and you may be
able to see over 100 miles to the San
Francisco Peaks near Flagstaff. On other
days, dust or pollution limit the view
and dull the colors._

from the Petrified Forest to the Grand Canyon. Within the park two portions are preserved as wilderness. No roads penetrate this harsh land, an intriguing maze of hills and washes. Only by hiking can you experience the area on a personal scale.

Each season ▷ makes its presence known. Winter may leave its mark as a light dusting of frost, or cover the land with a thick blanket of white. Winter is quiet. Birds leave, lizards sleep, and cold winds keep all but the adventurous in their vehicles.

FRED HIRSCHMANN

▲ **Summer brings many changes. Early summer is hot. Dry winds scour the desert. As summer** progresses, monsoon rains begin and the afternoons are filled with dark skies, thunder, and lightning. Torrential downpours deliver half the year's total rainfall, quickly transforming dry washes into short-lived rivers. Summer is busy, both for the park staff and for park wildlife. Everything comes to life with the rains. The flowers bloom, and animals raise their young and gather food for the coming winter.

Climate—
Shaper of the Painted Desert

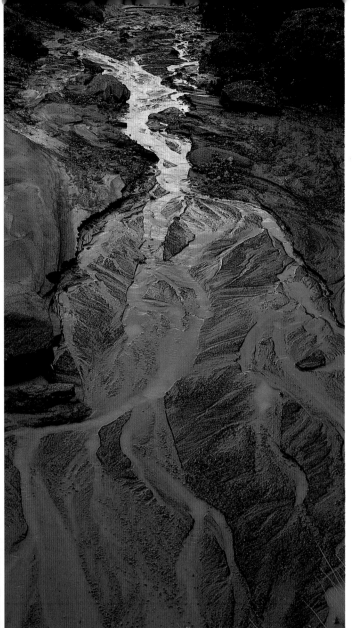

◁ **W**ater is the main force that shapes this land. The rain that nourishes sparse vegetation is the same rain that can gather to rip plants loose from a hillside. Strong rains can topple petrified logs and wash away tons of clay in a single storm. Though slower, winter moisture also shapes this land. Snow and ice, and the daily cycle of freeze and thaw, combine to break rocks apart.

FRED HIRSCHMANN

Water trickling through a sandy wash ▷ in the western Painted Desert is surrounded by the work of the seasons. Winter snows and ice have dissolved the cement holding these sculpted sandstone hoodoos together. Dry winds of spring and summer have carried the loosened sand grains away, smoothing the surface of the rocks. Late summer's thunderstorms have scoured the wash bottom, tumbling and abrading the rocks. Even the tiny trickle of water is carrying its load of fine clay particles.

◁ **Sandstone** hoodoos stand below Blue Mesa. Harder sandstone caprocks have protected them from the erosive powers of water.

△ **Left behind as water and wind** carried away finer sand and clay particles, colorful pebbles of chert and petrified wood lie scattered on the desert floor.

Centuries of frost and ▷ thunderstorms have smoothed and rounded these boulders at Blue Mesa.

Other Forms and Shapes

These alternating ▷ hard and soft layers were once Triassic river sandbars. Today the layers are carved into fanciful figures in remote areas of the Painted Desert.

FRED HIRSCHMANN

Water has already begun ▽ to shape this freshly exposed sandstone layer, attacking it along regularly spaced cracks. These are the hoodoos of the future.

KIRKENDALL/SPRING

◁ **Triassic rivers of 225 million** years ago carried sand into the Blue Mesa area. Groundwater cemented the sand grains together into layers of sandstone. Today that process is reversed; rains dissolve the cements, and intermittent streams carry the sand away. This melting sandstone ledge reminds us that nature is never static, its cycles are endless.

◁ *The Painted Desert Inn is a blending of cultures and styles. The exterior combines Spanish and Pueblo styles while harmonizing with the pinks of the Painted Desert.*

RUSS FINLEY

▽ **Built as a tourist stop in the 1920s, the Painted Desert Inn has always enjoyed a spectacular view of** *the surrounding landscape. After the Inn, and a portion of the Painted Desert, were added to the park in 1932, the Civilian Conservation Corps began enlarging and extensively remodeling the structure. Food, souvenirs, and the view made it a popular stop with travelers on Route 66. Today, it remains a good place to relax and escape the pace of the highway.*

The blending of ▷
southwestern traditions
continues in the trading
post room. The furnishings
and hammered-tin light
fixtures follow Mexican
designs, while the hand-
painted skylight panels are
based on ancient
southwestern Indian
pottery motifs.

FRED HIRSCHMANN

▲ **Civilian Conservation Corps**
workers spent the first winter cutting
timbers from nearby forests to form the
beams (vigas and sabinos) that were
used in the ceiling. With hand tools
they cut the capitals which top the
columns in a style that continued
the Spanish influence.

FRED HIRSCHMANN

Hopi artist Fred Kabotie was commissioned ▲
in 1948 to paint several murals in the Inn. Mr. Kabotie
was a driving force in the revitalization of Hopi arts
and crafts. He drew on the traditions of the Hopi
people to produce murals that reflect their culture and
connections to this Painted Desert country. This
depiction of the Buffalo Dance is in the old snack bar.
Like the Inn itself, this social dance represents a
blending of cultures. Originating with various Plains
tribes, it was traded among many tribes
throughout the southwest.

The Earliest People

Over 500 archaeological sites lie scattered throughout Petrified Forest, an irreplaceable record of those who lived here for thousands of years. At first glance, the lives of these early people may seem strange and very different from ours, but a second look reveals similarities as well as differences. Like us, these people needed food, shelter, and ways to share their thoughts, concerns, and feelings. Through careful study, archaeologists can help us understand both the differences and the similarities. Projectile points, planting sticks, and grinding stones provide clues to diet. Pithouses, pueblos, and campsites demonstrate adaptability in providing shelter. The locations of ruins and artifacts hint at social organization. Petroglyphs and pottery fragments show artistic skills and forms of expression that are still admired today. From pottery fragments to large pueblos, from flakes of petrified wood to huge panels of petroglyphs, each clue brings us closer to an understanding of the lives of these people.

▲ *This small projectile point* may have killed a bird, a rabbit, or some other small game, adding variety to a diet that was based on three staples: squash, beans, and corn.

▽ *Just as our homes reveal our personalities, the remains* of Puerco Village help us understand its inhabitants. Rows of rooms enclosed a central plaza that bustled with activity. The small rooms were saved for storage, sleeping, and to escape the elements.

Petroglyphs, or rock inscriptions, ▷ are common throughout Petrified Forest but Newspaper Rock has an unusually dense concentration. What thoughts and messages were these people expressing?

As They Left Their Mark

◁ **C**oarse stones for coarse seeds, fine stones for fine grains. How many hours were spent here each day grinding wild seeds and corn for the family?

RUSS FINLEY

Pottery and ▷ petrified wood were both shaped by the Western Pueblo People. Flakes of petrified wood produced sharp tools, while pottery was formed into countless shapes for cooking and storage.

◁ **D**esert varnish is a dark thin coating of iron or mangane that slowly forms on the rock surface. Petroglyphs are made by chipping through this coat to reveal the light rock beneath.

FRED HIRSCHMANN

△ **W**hile the artist probably saw a bird catch a toad, modern eyes often interpret this petroglyph differently.

Hiking in the Painted Desert ▷ wilderness may offer glimpses of unexpected messages from the past.

FRED HIRSCHMANN

◁ **T**he exact meanings of petroglyphs remain unclear. Some track the change of seasons, some resemble modern clan symbols, but most are left entirely for interpretation by the viewer.

39

Petrified Forest Today

Since 1906, the Petrified Forest has been protected, first as a national monument and, since 1962, as a national park. Although it was originally established to protect the outstanding fossils, there is much more to today's park. Since the park is a wildlife sanctuary protected from grazing, the grasslands that so impressed early explorers have now returned. Each spring brings birth and rebirth to the landscape as plants and animals welcome the new year. The slower processes of erosion gradually reshape the land. With most human developments excluded from the park, the wide vistas associated with the West have remained wide here. But Petrified Forest is still not immune to the changes that occur in and around it. Today, close to a million people visit the park every year. Each of those visitors must tread softly to avoid causing even small impacts that could scar the land and its resources. Development and air pollution must now narrow the wide vistas. Our actions must harmonize with nature's cycles. People come here to learn, to relax, and to enjoy, whether as scientist or as tourist. The park is a sanctuary not only for the natural world and the processes that shape it, but also for us. It is a link to our Earth.

RUSS FINLEY

◁ △ **A**lthough nature should rule in a national park, it is hard to resist lending a hand. This 1898 photograph (right), hand-colored by F. H. Maude, shows Agate Bridge eight years before Petrified Forest National Monument was established. In the early 1900s, people feared the bridge would collapse, so concrete supports were constructed (left). Would Agate Bridge have fallen without these supports? Yes, but geologic time moves slowly, and no one could know when it would fall. Was the preservation of this bridge worth the price of its current disfigurement?

▲ **The cool, clear air and rich colors of early morning are an irresistible lure to many who want to see** the Painted Desert at its best. Photographers seek to capture the scene on film. Others watch for wildlife before animals seek shelter against the hot, dry day to follow. Hikers and scientists use this time to "beat the heat." Each new day offers a wealth of surprises and enjoyment amid the badlands and plains of the park.

◁ **Mariposa lilies** seem particularly fragile when discovered beside a petrified log. The desert is truly a land of contrasts.

△ **Moisture is never easy to find in the** Painted Desert. Creamy-blossomed yuccas depend on a deep taproot for water.

◁ **Pronghorn have made an excellent recovery** since their brush with extinction near the turn of the century. Natural areas like Petrified Forest are important to their continued success.

△ **Most** park visitors never see a porcupine or a fox, even though both live here. On the other hand, lizards are everywhere. Desert creatures have specific requirements that allow them to survive, requirements that may make it easy, or difficult, for our paths to cross. Collared lizards are especially conspicuous, using the summer sun to warm themselves so they can pursue their prey. When this hunter becomes hunted, the collared lizard makes a two-legged sprint, looking like a little dinosaur.

Life in the Desert Scene

Feathers fluffed against a ▷
morning chill, the horned lark is a
year-round park resident.

STEPHEN TRIMBLE

JAMES TALLON

The rangy black-tailed △ ▷
jackrabbit and the plump Desert cottontail
both live in the park, but lead different
lives. When threatened, the cottontail will
make a quick dash for cover. The
jackrabbit will escape with a bounding lope
that easily outdistances its predators.

◁ **M**ore park
flowers bloom after
the late summer
rains than during
the drier springtime.
In August, golden
buckwheat
becomes a mound
of yellow flowers,
especially on the
volcanic soils of the
Painted Desert rim.

Like other ▷ *areas of the park, the barren landscape of the Tepees seems incapable of supporting life. But by avoiding the heat, hoarding water, selecting favorable sites, and adapting their behavior to the realities of the environment, plants and animals can prosper here.*

LARRY ULRICH

Petrified Forest Museum Association

In 1941, a group of Holbrook businessmen established the Petrified Forest Museum Association, an organization that has proven a lasting benefit for the park and its visitors. Proceeds from the association's visitor center bookstores and active publishing program support park preservation and interpretation, fund scientific investigations, print handouts for park visitors, and purchase needed equipment. By 1991, assistance from the association had topped $1 million.

SUGGESTED READING

ASH, SIDNEY. *Petrified Forest: The Story Behind the Scenery.* Petrified Forest National Park: Petrified Forest Museum Association, 1985.

COLBERT, EDWIN H. and R. ROY JOHNSON, editors. *The Petrified Forest Through the Ages.* Flagstaff, Arizona: Museum of Northern Arizona, Bulletin 54, 1985.

HOUK, ROSE. *The Painted Desert: Land of Light and Shadow.* Petrified Forest National Park: Petrified Forest Museum Association, 1990.

LONG, ROBERT and ROSE HOUK. *Dawn of the Dinosaurs: The Triassic in Petrified Forest.* Petrified Forest National Park: Museum Association, 1988.

TRIMBLE, STEPHEN. *Earth Journey, A Road Guide to Petrified Forest.* Petrified Forest National Park: Petrified Forest Museum Association, 1984.

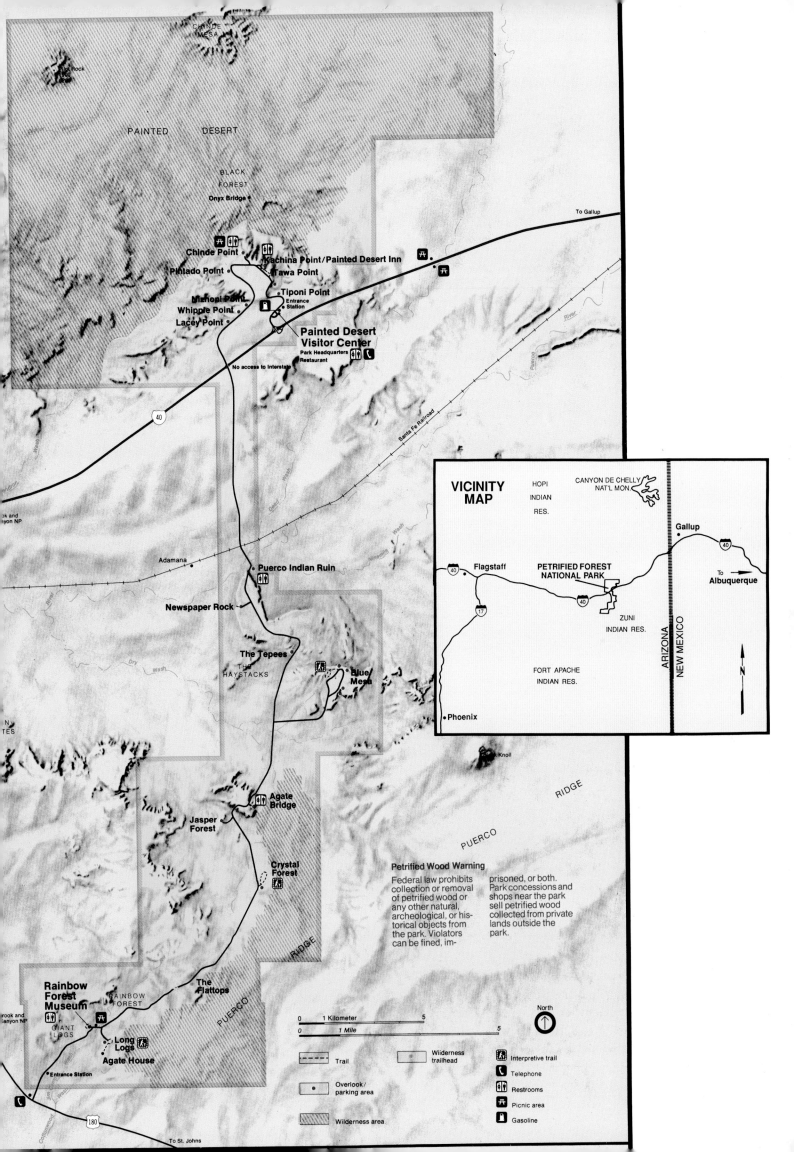

PAINTED DESERT

BLACK FOREST

Onyx Bridge

Chinde Point

Kachina Point/Painted Desert Inn

Piñado Point

Tawa Point

Tiponi Point

Mishopi Point

Entrance Station

Whipple Point

Lacey Point

To Gallup

**Painted Desert
Visitor Center**

Park Headquarters
Restaurant

No access to Interstate

40

Santa Fe Railroad

Adamana

Puerco Indian Ruin

Newspaper Rock

The Tepees

THE HAYSTACKS

Blue Mesa

VICINITY MAP

HOPI INDIAN RES.

CANYON DE CHELLY NAT'L MON.

Gallup

40

Flagstaff

**PETRIFIED FOREST
NATIONAL PARK**

To
Albuquerque

17

40

ZUNI INDIAN RES.

ARIZONA

NEW MEXICO

FORT APACHE INDIAN RES.

Phoenix

N

Knoll

RIDGE

PUERCO

Agate Bridge

Jasper Forest

Crystal Forest

Petrified Wood Warning

Federal law prohibits collection or removal of petrified wood or any other natural, archeological, or historical objects from the park. Violators can be fined, im-prisoned, or both. Park concessions and shops near the park sell petrified wood collected from private lands outside the park.

RIDGE

PUERCO

Rainbow Forest Museum

RAINBOW FOREST

The Flattops

Brook and Canyon NP

GIANT LOGS

Long Logs

Agate House

Entrance Station

North

0   1 Kilometer   5

0   1 Mile   5

180

To St. Johns

- - - - Trail

Wilderness trailhead

Interpretive trail

Overlook/
parking area

Telephone

Restrooms

Wilderness area

Picnic area

Gasoline

On December 8, 1906, Teddy Roosevelt signed a proclamation establishing Petrified Forest as the nation's second national monument. In 1958, Congress passed a bill that elevated the monument to a national park in 1962. This corner of the Painted Desert didn't change because of those actions. What changed was our attitude toward this land. The petrified wood, bones, and other fossils became more than just curiosities; they are keys to understanding the evolution of life. Scattered ruins and potsherds offer glimpses of an earlier life here. The land itself, the barren clays of the desert, the grasses and shrubs of the plains, the animals that live here—all are resources to be studied and perpetuated. What has made, and what will keep, the Petrified Forest special, is the care that we show it. Only through our care can the gift given us by those who have gone before be passed on to those who will follow.

GAIL BANDINI

Agate House was home to the Western Pueblo People. How did their relationship to this land differ from ours?

47

FRED HIRSCHMANN

▲ *"The petrified logs are countless at all horizons...while the ground seems to be everywhere studded with gems consisting of the broken fragments of all shapes and sizes and exhibiting all the colors of the rainbow." Paleontologist Lester F. Ward, U.S. Geological Survey, 1899.*

Inside back cover: At ▷ Blue Mesa, the daily cycle continues as night approaches. Photo by Fred Hirschmann.

Back cover: Jasper ▷ Forest is strewn with fragments of a distant past. Photo by Randy A. Prentice.

Books in this "in pictures ... The Continuing Story" series are: Arches & Canyonlands, Bryce Canyon, Death Valley, Everglades, Glacier, Glen Canyon-Lake Powell, Grand Canyon, Grand Teton, Hawai`i Volcanoes, Mount Rainier, Mount St. Helens, Olympic, Petrified Forest, Rocky Mountain, Sequoia & Kings Canyon, Yellowstone, Yosemite, Zion.

Translation Packages are also available. Each title can be ordered with a booklet in German, or French, or Japanese bound into the center of the English book. Selected titles in this series as well as other KC Publications' books are available in up to five additional languages.

The original national park series, "The Story Behind the Scenery," covers over 75 parks and related areas. A series on Indian culture is also available. To receive our catalog listing over 90 titles:
Call (800-626-9673), fax (702-433-3420), or write to the address below.

───────────────

Published by KC Publications, 3245 E. Patrick Ln., Suite A, Las Vegas, NV 89120.

Created, Designed and Published in the U.S.A.
Printed by Dong-A Publishing and Printing, Seoul, Korea
Color Separations by Kedia/Kwangyangsa Co., Ltd.